Liberté,

Égalité,

Fraternité?

First published 2020 by The Hedgehog Poetry Press

Published in the UK by
The Hedgehog Poetry Press
5, Coppack House
Churchill Avenue
Clevedon
BS21 6QW

www.hedgehogpress.co.uk

ISBN: 978-1-913499-59-4

Copyright © Mark Davidson 2020

The right of Mark Davidson to be identified as the editor of this work has been asserted in accordance with the Copyright, Designs and Patents Act 1988. All rights for individual works retained by the respective author.

All rights reserved. No part of this publication may be reproduced, stored in or introduced into a retrieval system, or transmitted in any form, or by any means (electronic, mechanical, photocopying, recording or otherwise) without prior written permissions of the publisher. Any person who does any unauthorised act in relation to this publication may be liable for criminal prosecution and civil claims for damages,

9 8 7 6 5 4 3 2 1

A CIP Catalogue record for this book is available from the British Library.

Poems of Liberté by Elisabeth Kelly

Week 1: The Beginning 7
Week 2: Changing States of matter 8
Week 3: Stabilisation of States 9
Week 4: Exploration of Atoms 10
Week 5: Another Beginning 11

Poems of Égalité by Kate Young

Opposites Attract 15
Indigo Moons 16
Nirvana from Inside a Van 17
Display Case in Red 18
The Day of Reckoning 19

Poems of Fraternité by Mick Yates

spring 23
tending the flowers 24
when the blackbird sings at dawn 25
conversing with bees 26
coronavirus 27

Poems of
Liberté

by

Elisabeth Kelly

WEEK 1: THE BEGINNING

Air was compressing around us,
I took you by the hand
and we ran.

I caught the dense sky and
wrapped it around us

It's too tight you said.
It has to be I whispered.

WEEK 2: CHANGING STATES OF MATTER

They sky lay on our bodies
like mercury caught in a loop,
changing state.
Transforming every
second.

Liquid, solid, gas.

We watched.
Transfixed.

WEEK 3: STABILISATION OF STATES

We swam in the liquid,
it spread over our backs,
seeking out creases in our sun
tightened skin.

We swallowed in the gas,
youthful inflating breaths,
making us giddy with oxygen.

We scrambled up the solid mass.
Laughingly skinned our knees on the way.
Looked down at the changing earth,
seasons played out one field at a time.

WEEK 4: EXPLORATION OF ATOMS

The world stood still.
The cloud shadows,
on the neighbouring hills
stopped moving.
We watched the grass crackle,
we caught grasshoppers.

Air particles,
molecules, atoms, quarks
stood still in a vacuum.
We plucked them out,
perfect in their completion, in their stillness
we turned them round, mixed them up
put them back.

My mind slowly unfurled and I let
go of your hands.

WEEK 5: ANOTHER BEGINNING

There is a pace now
to our days.
A gentle rhythm of
completeness.

We have folded in,
tucked the corners
around our life.

We have expanded,
contracted.

Found contentment.

Poems of Égalité

by

Kate Young

OPPOSITES ATTRACT

In this uneven universe I create stability,
for I am the Goddess of parity
cupping the weight of consideration
softly in each balanced palm,
rolling opinion, ripe with expectation
rounded as sumptuous fruit.

All things being equal
I peel away skins of indecision
and when replete with deliberation
turn, slightly out of kilter,
scales laid bare
mouthing my calculation wordlessly.

For in all shadow I see light,
trading new-borns sliding from womb
for the dried-up gasping veins of age.
I am division, solidarity,
equilibrium, polarity
your world poised in my hand.

INDIGO MOONS

Drawn by monotonous magnetic pull
the women in black,
the hunched and the hungry
are dragged down into indigo seas
carrying mis-shapen moons on their backs
traipse, toil, rub, cleanse,
rinse, wring, fold, roll,
laundry swelling, waxing expectant.

They do not complain
the women in black,
the hunched and the hungry
trudging slowly in single file
howling in silence like wolves in the tide
their violet voices silenced by mountains
windowed cells hauling them back
calling for curfew, return to the cage.

NIRVANA FROM INSIDE A VAN

She turns,
bones rattle
on base of transit.

In Eden, rosary fruit
tumbles gently
its soft dong spilt, lilting.

She weeps,
bloodied nails
scraping fear from metal cage.

In bejewelled lagoon
wounds are soothed,
waters whispering sadly.

She inhales,
nostrils weeping tears
of urine and sweat.

Fragrant frankincense,
sweet as oiled waters
bathes tired feet.

She slides
under darkness so deep
it blackens Hope's face.

Familiar features
hang from portrait tree
smiling like the blessed.

Journey ends
twisting like Styx in city streets
Icarus eyes drawn to light.

shimmering opals
dance in pools
of feathered flight.

Shredded wings falter
scrambling documents carried
close as a promise.

She rolls
a slither in an alley,
coins clink, exchanging glances.

DISPLAY CASE IN RED

She slumps
spreading herself on a bed of red
in an airless
light deprived cell
eyes fixed
in perfect stillness

a once exotic butterfly
netted
encased
pinned and displayed
awkwardly
legs unfolded
splayed unaturally
centred
poised
for one last immobile flight.

What drew her here
dragged her down
as she emerged from cocoon
uncomfortable in her wings?

She no longer recognises
this anonymous woman
inert
turned to mirror
eyes fixed
dead
spread across a bed of red
in perfect stillness.

THE DAY OF RECKONING

From a Dublin hotel she considers
the empty scale hung from hand,
eyes fixed on strands of beads
dangling over edges of thoughts.

Light glances off folds of cloth
concealing a secret, tight as a knot,
her belly swollen as the Liffey in May
spring rain following tidal lines.

She has contacts, faceless names
skilled in the art of disposal
who, with the ease of a scalpel,
could slice through cord heavy with guilt.

No, she will wait for time to roll over,
force anonymity into the world.
A bundle will pass to expectant arms
leaving her, empty balance in hand.
.

Poems of

Fraternité

by

Mick Yates

SPRING

spring has arrived once more

bringing the promise of new life

amidst the carnage of the coronavirus plague

that is rampaging around our planet

i look at the daffodils by the river

gently dancing in the early morning breeze

i talk to them quietly and respectfully

i say to them 'i seek solace and answers to

some difficult questions that have been troubling me lately

like what is happening in the world?

will we survive? will we continue to live much longer?

is humanity doomed forever? what can i do to help mankind?

please tell me sweet daffodils please give me some hope'

they look tenderly back at me and smile saying

'we are truly sorry but we cannot help you

we are just daffodils enjoying the warmth of the spring sun'

TENDING THE FLOWERS

i watch my partner in life
gently spraying water
on the flowers she has so carefully
planted earlier this year
so much care and so much tenderness
involved in giving and nurturing life
i wonder about this world of ours
which at times seems so devoid of love
we do not really care about each other
we are always divided and at odds with ourselves
on a personal a national and a global level
rich and poor black and white
people against people nation against nation
in our diversity lies the source of our conflict
our wars our indifference our cruelty
but in our shared common heritage
lies our salvation for the future
let us learn a lesson from flowers
and all the other glorious splendours
that life has to offer on this planet
before it is too late to save our world

WHEN THE BLACKBIRD SINGS AT DAWN

i do not know

what the blackbird sings

for i do not understand

either the lyrics or the tune

it is such a sweet song though

so melodious and full of hope

that any deeper understanding seems irrelevant

he gently serenades me

as i lie in bed in the early morning

he sings i am certain

only about the good things in life

those that lift my spirits

and banish my dark thoughts

he seems content just to be alive

as the passing night slides into a new day

CONVERSING WITH BEES

it is a hot summer day

i am sitting by the river

in one of my uncertain moods

considering the imponderables of existence

like what is the meaning of life?

while searching for answers

i watch the honey bees at work

hovering from flower to flower

humming happily as they go about their business

'what is the meaning of life?' i enquire of them

'we are really not bothered much

about the imponderables of existence' they answer

'we are merely bees moving from flower

seeking out the sweet nectar of life'

CORONAVIRUS

when all this has passed

when all this is old news and long forgotten

when we reflect upon it all

let us not remember the isolation

the need to separate ourselves from others

the fear of being with friends

or in the company of strangers

the dread of selfish avarice

the terror of being without food

the sheer futility of such a life

when this is all over

let us embrace all that it means to be human

let us understand that as individuals

we are part of a living community

that we have families and children

that we have friends and neighbours

that the world is a small fragile place

and that life is tenuous in truth

we are here for a reason

and that reason is to embrace others

and to love all of humanity

ELISABETH KELLY

Elisabeth Kelly has recently returned to poetry writing. She lives on a hill farm in the Scottish Borders with her young family and too many animals. She has had poems accepted for publication by Dreich Magazine, Foxglove Journal and was Shortlisted in the Anthony Cronin International Poetry Award 2020. She loves the change of seasons and chocolate puddings.

Thank you to Damian, Heather and Leo for all their love and support and Claire F for her faith right at the start.

KATE YOUNG

Kate Young grew up in Norwich, Norfolk where she completed her teaching qualification. She moved to Chatham, Kent in 1978 to start a long teaching career and still enjoys the odd day working with KS1. She lives with her husband, her grown-up children having 'flown the nest'! She has been passionate about poetry and literature since childhood. She generally writes free verse and loves responding to Art through Ekphrastic poems. If pushed, she would name TS Eliot as her favourite poet.

Her work has appeared in *Ninemuses, Ekphrastic Review, Nitrogen House, Words for the Wild and Poetry on the Lake*. She has poems due to be included in a Scottish Writers Centre chapbook and an anthology taken from the Places of Poetry project last year. She is a member of her local Poetry Society Stanza and the Poetry Society of the Open University.

Find her on Twitter @Kateyoung12poet.

Acknowledgements:

Indigo Moons- appeared in *Ekphrastic Review* April 2019

Opposites Attract- also in *Ekphrastic Review* April 2019

Display Case in Red- appeared in *Nine Muses* April 2019

MICK YATES

Mick Yates lives in the far north of England. He has worked extensively as a playwright and has had more than thirty plays produced at theatres across the country. He has received many awards, including an Edinburgh Festival Fringe First. He has also written for television, most notably for the BBC series *Doctors*. His debut poetry collection *artefacts* won the 2014 Geoff Stevens Memorial Poetry Prize and it was published by Indigo Dreams Publishing in 2015. His second collection *kaleidoscope* was published by them in 2017. A new chapbook, *the art of conversation*, was published by the New York based Clare Songbirds Publishing House in 2018.

Another collection *the shapes of passion* was also published by Clare Songbirds Publishing House in 2018 to be followed by *random thoughts from the north* which was published by them in 2019. His most recent collection *the blue hour* was published by The Hedgehog Poetry Press in 2019. He was longlisted in 2017, 2018 and 2019 for Best Poetry Pamphlet in the prestigious Saboteur Awards, and was also a Pushcart Prize nominee in 2018. His latest pamphlet *poems from egypt* was published by Barley Cottage Publications in February 2020 to be followed by *forever in eden* and *a river runs through here* in April 2020.

www.ingramcontent.com/pod-product-compliance
Lightning Source LLC
Chambersburg PA
CBHW021455080526
44588CB00009B/858